McSWEENEY'S
SAN FRANCISCO

Copyright © 2018 McSweeney's Publishing and the contributors. ASSISTED BY: Eric Cromie, Jane Rebecca Marchant, Ben Parker, Stephanie Steinbrecher. MANIFESTO SERIES EDITOR: Kristina Kearns. ONLINE EDITOR: Chris Monks. ART DIRECTOR: Sunra Thompson. EDITOR: Daniel Levin Becker. PROFOUND THANKS: Dave Eggers, Adam Werbach.

"This Bigness and This Whiteness" contains a passage from Amiri Baraka (LeRoi Jones), *Black Magic: Sabotage, Target Study, Black Art; Collected Poetry, 1961-1967* (The Bobbs-Merrill Company, 1969).

"Politically Correct? Hear Me Out, Please" contains an epigraph from Audre Lorde, *Our Dead Behind Us* (W. W. Norton & Company, 1986).

"Never Forget, Never Remember" contains a passage from M. Scott Peck, *The Different Drum: Community Making and Peace* (Touchstone, 1987).

Printed in the United States.

ISBN 978-1-944211-61-5

10 9 8 7 6 5 4 3 2 1

www.mcsweeneys.net

SMALL BLOWS AGAINST ENCROACHING TOTALITARIANISM

Volume One

The Manifesto Series
McSweeney's Books

A LAND GOVERNED BY UNKINDNESS REAPS NO KINDNESS

by Terrance Hayes

I commit to vote because a land governed by unkindness reaps no kindness. A land governed by fire finds no rain. I commit to vote because a land governed by the self-righteous is rarely right. A land governed by bloodshed sheds blood, a land governed by the drowned will have nothing but rain for as long as the drowned reign. "I pick up my axe & fight like a farmer," Jimi Hendrix sings in "Machine Gun." I commit to vote because I will not love a land where belief has the same status as truth, a land where property means more than building. I will not love a land governed by men with coins covering their eyes, men with trunks for mouths, without ears, with clogged snouts and scales, rulers, sabers, flags. A land governed by madness is mad. "I pick up my axe & fight like a farmer." A land where helmets crawl over the hills and men emerge from the earth covered in exhaustion is a land whose energy is made of suffering. I commit to vote because I will not love a land governed by someone who has never made his own bed, who has never made anything but money. I commit to vote because any intelligent person has to fear when someone with no respect for authority has authority.

THE WIDENING GYRE
by Tom Bissell

America used to be the well-meaning but erratic guy who arrives at a party already drunk and proceeds to down three bourbons, tell an arguably racist joke, shove a waiter, and end up vomit-crying in the bathroom while his appalled friends pat him on the back and tell him it'll be okay. We got away with the geopolitical equivalent of this behavior for more than a century, and it worked out for us, mostly, though less so for everyone else. Today, however, America is the guy who arrives at an AA meeting twenty minutes late, high on meth, waving around a loaded antique Luger, all while his stripper girlfriend sits outside in a 1986 Dodge Caravan, hashtagging her latest Instagram post #blessed.

It's not too late to change this. We can ensure, at the very least, the rebanishing of Donald J. Trump to ribbon-cuttings for luxury high-rises that won't get built and signings for books he didn't write. But after that we'll have to do the hard thing, which is accept that Trump is not an aberration of the American character but its pornographically erumpent apotheosis. As I write these words, 40 percent of my fellow Americans maintain their support for the president and his policies–his turning and turning effect on the widening American gyre. As most sensitive, sensible people are currently asking themselves: *How in the sweet name of Christ is this possible?*

I hail from the American heartland. Most of my extended family voted for Trump, as did probably 80 percent of the people I was close to growing up. Current pollster orthodoxy holds that Trump was propelled into this calamitous presidency by the benighted souls of Forgotten America, which is to say the America I grew up in. It's not like this is wrong: Delta County, Michigan, in which I'm still registered to vote, went for Trump 69 to 24 percent. I'm told by those who've studied the issue that Forgotten Americans experienced the Obama era as a long, painful gauntlet of demographic anxiety and alienation from their own culture. I hear laments on liberal podcasts about how the Democratic Party, or the Left generally, ignored Forgotten Americans at its own electoral peril–and is now reaping a whirlwind of neglect. But then I hear other, less patient commentators proclaim that most Forgotten Americans are rancid bigots anyway, so to hell with them.

Needless to say, the complicated sociological phenomenon of Trumpism is not likely to be explained, much less solved, by a single equation. But the night Trump won, I sat there, in a North Dakota hotel room, blinking at my computer screen with one memory in my head, the elucidatory power of which has only grown over the last year. It was 1997 and I was twenty-three years old. I had just climbed into a taxicab in the former Soviet Union—Tashkent, Uzbekistan, to be precise—and found myself staring at a lovingly framed picture of Josef Stalin on the dashboard. The driver, an ethnic Russian, was quite old, so I knew he'd likely grown up in the shadow of the Great Terror, wherein tens of millions of innocent Soviets were rounded up and sent to the gulag (if they were lucky) or unceremoniously executed (if they were not). This shameful chapter of history, as well as Stalin's complicity with it, was widely known within the Soviet Union by the 1960s and openly discussed by the 1990s.

I was just learning Russian, and because I liked to practice my language skills with new people, but also because I wondered how any human being could publicly idolize Stalin, I asked the old man about the portrait. He said a bunch of things I didn't understand, but one thing

I understood perfectly: "Yes, he did bad things. But he made us feel strong."

The former-Soviet world of the 1990s was filled with millions of confused, angry people, most of them stripped of the certainties of an ideology and identity they'd spent their lives inhabiting. There would be no Vladimir Putin today without those confused, angry people reaching back in search of vanished strength. White America generally, but rural white America specifically, believes it is facing an equally existential threat. It's not, obviously, but everything from freely available opioids to the bloviation of Sean Hannity to the insectoid hivewar of Facebook exacerbates the grave cultural danger they believe they're in. Our fellow Americans thus reached back into the fog and found their hands around the unlikely savior of Donald J. Trump. Yes, he does bad things. They know that. But he makes them feel strong.

Frightened, angry people are not known for making sensible choices. With the election of Donald Trump, millions of Americans made what is arguably the least sensible choice in our nation's electoral history. We could choose to yell at them for that, shame them, or even fight them, and maybe that's what they deserve. But what we deserve as Americans—what we all deserve—is not a future of kakistocracy, Great Leader personality cults, and blood-and-soil nativism, but rather the continuation of the idea we were all once taught to believe in: a tolerant, generous, diverse nation founded upon ideals it has not always lived up to.

Right now, those ideals have never been more imperiled—or more relevant. Many Trump supporters know they've done something indefensible in electing him, but our pain and confusion make it all worth it. But the rest of them, the non-nihilists (or "non-deplorables," if you will), they're looking for something to believe in, just like the rest of us. They want a future for their children, just like the rest of us. If we who oppose Trump are not, in every way, better than Trump—more forgiving, more friendly, more generous, more welcoming, more humble, more circumspect about what we cannot hope to know—he will win. If his supporters can look at our side and see nothing but anger and resentment, he will win. I don't mean he wins the next election cycle, though he well may. I mean he'll finally succeed in creating a vacuum of hope and goodwill, which is all it takes for authoritarian longing to flourish. And then his final perversion of America will be complete.

ATTACK OF THE SHINY BLACK OXFORD

by Dodie Bellamy

I commit to vote because when I close my eyes in a gesture of "active imagination"–an activity I considered really stupid when I actually was in therapy, and I was horrible at it, but now I see plenty–I see a slug on a sidewalk, its tentacles trembling as a shiny black leather Oxford looms above it, slowly descending in a grinding motion. The slug says to me, "This is how precarious it feels to live in America today." The slug says, "Ignore those on the radical left who post online that Democrats are as bad as Republicans, so it's a moral imperative to opt out of the system and refuse to vote." Of course capitalism is oppressive and corrupt–this past year since Trump was elected, we can feel that in our gut–and perhaps that gut sense of systemic wrongness is the only good thing Trump has given us. We all know the Democrats aren't going to get rid of capitalism any time soon, and they're not going to lead us to a paradise where slugs frolic in moist earth with delectable rotting vegetation to feed on. But maybe they can halt this apocalyptic momentum that's traumatizing living beings and their environments.

I've only seen slugs once, a few weeks after the Loma Prieta earthquake in 1989. My cat Stanley fell or jumped out of a window and went missing for three weeks. Then one evening as I was doing the dishes, staring vacantly into the backyard of the building next door, I saw these two eyes gleaming in the darkness. I ran outside, but nothing would get Stanley to come to me. So I rented a humane trap from this guy in Oakland who called me "Babe" and snuck it into the neighbor's backyard. I armed the trap with a bowl of cat food to make it more enticing, and I waited. Later, when I checked, there was no Stanley, but the bowl was swarming with slugs. They were disgusting. But so resourceful. When attacked, a slug contracts its soft watery body, hardening it into a still, round ball. Slugs exude slippery foul-tasting mucus that makes them difficult to catch. In a pinch some of them will amputate their own tails, like the Spartan warriors. In arid conditions, a desert slug can hibernate for years, waiting for moisture to revitalize it. Despite its lack of shell, when pushed too far, a slug will attack. My imaginary slug burps up a wad of slime and says, "We've got to get rid of that Oxford or it's going to squish our guts in a big splat. Get off your complacent consumerist ass and vote Democrat in 2018!" The next night my cat Stanley beat the slugs to the food, and he lived a long healthy life until 2002.

HOW CAN YOU NOT SEE THIS?

by Lev Grossman

I don't talk about politics a lot, at least not publicly. I don't write about politics much either. I justify this to myself with the argument that I write fiction, and fiction promotes empathy, and critical thinking, and ideological skepticism. It strengthens whatever mental muscles you use to see other people's points of view. It's deeper and more fundamental than politics. Once you taint it with politics, you've already lost.

This may or may not be true. But it makes me feel a bit better.

Nevertheless I think about politics a lot. A lot of this thinking takes the form of conversations with imaginary Trump supporters where we talk about the president and what he's doing.

It's become a pretty elaborate fantasy. It's actually escalated to the point where in my head I regularly host an imaginary talk show, where a liberal Democrat and a conservative Republican come on and discuss hot-button issues like gun control or immigration or climate change or economic inequality. I'm the host of the show. I'm also the liberal Democrat. (Sorry, but look, it's my fantasy.) Whenever the guests disagree over a fact or a point of law, there's a bipartisan panel of experts there to try to clear it up.

The only rule on my fantasy show is that no one's allowed to get angry. You can talk about your values, you can make arguments, you can cite facts, the Bible, whatever; you just can't get pissed off. If you get pissed off then you're kicked off the show. (I actually think this is a really good idea, by the way. Hollywood, call me!)

I spend a lot of time saying–mentally, in character as the liberal Democrat–things like *How can you not see this? How*–for example–can you forget that only a few years ago we had a massive financial crisis because a lot of rich people were getting richer by selling fraudulent financial instruments, which they could do because their industry was under-regulated? That when the hoax failed the American people bailed them out with our own tax dollars, then put in place regulations to make sure it didn't happen again? And now those same plutocrats, in the form of Trump and his cabinet, are dismantling these regulations and telling us it's for our own good? How can you believe them? How? *How?*

But at the same time I'm haunted by the sound—coming from the other side of the thin partition that divides this country—of literally millions of other people asking me the same thing, in exactly the same tone of voice, from the opposite side of the argument. *How can you not understand?* They are as incredulous about my political convictions as I am about theirs. What on earth has happened? It's as though America's timeline forked, but incompletely, so that two divergent countries are stuck in the same universe, sloppily superimposed on each other. And the inhabitants are all mightily pissed off at each other.

I take the opinions of the right seriously. I could not in good conscience dispense with or discard the passionate opinions of millions of Americans who disagree with me. I have no patience for the name-calling and appearance-mocking and gotcha-smugness that come from both sides of the aisle. And I think I recognize the extent to which the media I consume is biased. (I worked for *Time* magazine for twenty years. I know how the news sausage is made.) I don't like taking sides in an America that is already bitterly divided and pitted against itself.

But the trouble is that reality, as the saying goes, has a well-known liberal bias. The facts, or the closest thing I can get to them, tell me that this country is in real and terrible danger from its own executive branch. We're in danger of destroying our own habitat. Children are dying by gunfire every single day. Our health care system is terribly broken. We're in danger of destroying immigrant families, and consigning millions of people to lives of hard work that don't even get them above the poverty line. We're in danger of squandering vast wealth and decades' worth of international goodwill that we could be using to make the world better. The Trump administration's policies and decisions have been consistently and demonstrably selfish, greedy, hypocritical, childish, petty, cowardly, dishonest, cruel, racist, and criminally indifferent to the sufferings of others.

I can't watch that happening and stay silent. I just can't. That's why I wrote this essay.

THE WIDE WORLD
OF BELONGING

by Kao Kalia Yang

I was born in a refugee camp in Thailand in December of 1980. I was the runt of the babies born that year in that hungry place, in that uncertain time. Few thought I would survive.

The Hmong, my people, had just escaped from the genocide of the aftermath of America's secret war in Laos. The Central Intelligence Agency of the United States had commissioned thirty-two thousand Hmong men and boys to fight and die on America's behalf. Most of the soldiers were killed during the war. Many more civilians were slaughtered after the Americans left. I was born to a people who had fled from death and despair in the hopes of a chance at life.

I was born on four hundred borrowed acres, funded by the United Nations, surrounded by Thai men with guns, in a place where Hmong people got food three days a week and little girls like me often disappeared in the dark of night.

My playground was the stretch of my mother's sarong, the reach of my father's arm. My playmates were hungry cousins with dirty faces and stomachs round and hard. Together, we laughed and we cried in that place where we jostled for this thing that meant more to our parents than anything else: a chance at life.

The life that the adults were running toward was a life that began for many of us in America: a life where we could go to school, have food in our bellies, reach far beyond our meager heights. A life that has not been easy but has been possible.

In America, I grew up in the cold of Minnesota. My family and many other Hmong families lived in the housing projects, strong rectangles of concrete rising out of the earth, buildings meant to house soldiers returning from World War II. We went to school on the yellow buses beneath the moody, gray skies, stood in long lines waiting for our free and then reduced-price school lunches, walked in a fine line from the big classrooms to the little ones where we learned that *a* is the beginning of *apple* and *b* can build a word called *boy*.

In America, I became a young person who held promise, a shy girl who got good grades at school, took care of her younger brothers and sisters at night when their parents worked the night shift at the factories, and sensed something growing inside of her.

It began as a small lump in the back of my throat as I sat by the window carefully maneuvering sharp nail clippers around the thick edges of my grandmother's toenails and she talked to me of a past on the other side of the world, a once-upon-a-time orphan girl who became a healer, a shaman, a medicine woman; of a girl not so different from myself, a girl who would become an old woman, become she who loved me. The lump grew bigger and sank deeper on the late nights when I sat on the carpet with my mother's throbbing feet in my hands, massaging and massaging away the heated knots I felt beneath my fingers, and listened as she talked of her work in the factories, of the quotas, the supervisors in their white hats, and the cement underneath her feet that grew harder by the hour. It settled in my heart when my grandmother died, with no room of her own, all of her life gathered into thirteen tattered suitcases as she journeyed from the house of one child to the next.

We were the working poor in America. We lived in neighborhoods with old houses whose rotting steps led to hollowed doors, paint cracking on either side. We drove used cars that smelled like cigarettes. We wore clothes from the church basements, sizes all wrong. Christmas was Toys for Tots. Thanksgiving was Meals on Wheels. Our mothers and fathers struggled to balance budgets that never worked. Our grandmothers died illiterate, their stories told but not recorded. On paper, mine had nothing behind it but a lifetime of poverty and war, despair and death. Yet year by year, as we grew older, we grew stronger.

I graduated from college, an expensive private education made possible by scholarships and student loans with interest rates that didn't kick in until after graduation. For us, Carleton College was only forty minutes away from St. Paul, but it was as far away as our grandmother's stories about life on the other side of the world.

I graduated from graduate school, one of the fine Ivy Leagues that children like me did not know how to dream of but somehow a hard life in America had made possible thanks to fellowships and loans. My mother and father sat together at my graduation, in that sea of parents, their first time in New York City, hands twisting the graduation program, sweat dripping down their faces along with their tears. The ghost of my grandmother wandered close by on the fine brick-lined walks of the university, her hands behind her back.

I became a writer to write that lump inside my heart out into the world, to dress it up in sunshine, cover it in flowers, and send it far into the eastern skies, so that the sun that rises, day in and day out, will see us for who we are: the outcomes of hard lives, the beautiful ending they have been waiting for.

They–those who have died so we could be here, those who have brought us here and drenched us in their tears so we would not dry up and wither away, those who have worked here so we could imagine possibilities beyond ticking clocks, a world free from the ever-moving assembly lines. They, the people of our past, and they, the people of our futures. In us, our ancestors and our descendants meet. Each of us is more than just he, she, or me.

I became a writer to push the edges of what we mean to ourselves and to each other, to the wide world of belonging.

I will take action because when the Central Intelligence Agency of the United States of America came to the high mountains of Laos and commissioned the death of the Hmong men and boys, the women and children, those high-ranking men never envisioned a life like mine taking root on American soil. I will take action because despite the odds, I am here doing work I love and living a life I am committed to, and those odds and this life are made possible by the goodwill of a bigger world, a world that believes little girls deserve a chance to grow up and become women, and that women are far stronger than any intelligence agency, machine of state and death, on earth.

THE IDEA OF
REASONABLE DEBATE

by Owen King

The attack at Columbine High School took place almost twenty years ago. The Washington Post recently reported that, in the years since, "210,000 students have experienced gun violence at school." This is a horrific statistic. But it barely scratches the surface of the way guns have disfigured our American life.

Everytown For Gun Safety tells us that ninety-six Americans are killed, on average, by a gun every day. I'm truly sorry, but I have to ask you to do something appalling: I have to ask you to imagine a gymnasium filled with ninety-six people. Now imagine them being ripped apart by gunfire, every man and woman and child. Now imagine watching that happen–and then, tomorrow, walking through a doorway to the next gymnasium holding ninety-six people who are to be massacred. Day after day after day. This is the grotesque status quo the NRA would like us to accept as a fair price for the freedom to arm ourselves against the threat of a tyrannical government.

My daughter, who is eight and wore her favorite pants with bunny appliqués to school this morning, participates in regular safety drills that train her to hide silently in a corner of her classroom with her friends. This is her share of the NRA's price.

If you believe that the connection I'm making between the NRA and all gun deaths is unfair or hyperbolic, then why is our country's rate of gun deaths so enormously incommensurate with the rate found in other developed countries? There are 3.61 per 100,000 in the United States versus, for instance, .16 in Australia and .04 in the United Kingdom. The difference is obvious. The difference is the NRA and the lax gun laws it promotes.

There are so many problems in American life: vast economic inequality, systemic racism, the environmental collapse of our rivers and coasts, our antiquated political system, our inconsistent foreign policy, and more. They are all pressing issues and they are all complex. Gun control is also pressing but, by comparison, it is straightforward. We need universal background checks. We need a federal prohibition against military-style rifles. We need limits on magazine sizes. These are sensible regulations and that's why most Americans support them, including 72 percent of Republicans.

I cannot help feeling that the gun crisis is at the core of everything that ails our country. It defiles our national life. It makes the idea of reasonable debate seem absurd, because what population of reasonable people would consent to live this way, perpetually under fire? If we can deal with this one issue first—if Americans can elect representatives who will pass the gun-control laws that the majority of us want passed—then perhaps the many other deliberations we must undertake can begin in earnest.

THIS BIGNESS
AND THIS WHITENESS

by Harmony Holiday

It begins innocently enough, with peeking at the 'other' through these radioactive machines, mapping her passage from slave to citizen, other to blackstar, reducing her to a series of objectified gestures and calling that the understanding. And like every low-level accomplice, once you get by with the first missive, you're intoxicated, emboldened, have become the toxic spectator you once denounced as capitalism's most pernicious hypocrite. The one, gluttonously informed and soaked in privilege, who sits around being bohemian about the information, fetshizing society's every crisis over cocktails and at dead university events trying to be festive about their lifelessness. This performance escalates from glimpses and mumbling bohemianism to complete scopophilia, reading every left-leaning news item, fist pumping at *Democracy Now!* broadcasts over Bulletproof® coffee in the morning, reveling in liberal outrage from pretty couches that smell faintly of sex and incense, diplomacy and *SNL*. You even take off your shirt and do the Donald Glover dance for company sometimes, on your knees while standing up. On more mellow occasions you just sit around and watch his "This Is America" video on enormous flat screens and quote Amiri's "Poem Some People Will Have to Understand":

> We have awaited the coming of a natural
> phenomenon. Mystics and romantics, knowledgeable
> workers
> of the land.
>
> But none has come.
> (*Repeat*)
>   but none has come.
> Will the machinegunners please step forward?

You grow bloodthirsty for some doom you can see and obey beyond saying. The pleasure so many have been taking in watching a black man in confederate army trousers reenact state violence, as if it arouses him to some level of excellence to play what he once himself dubbed *big and white*, the fact that Donald Glover's violent escapade of a music video is being received as an ironic, maybe even cathartic, stroke of genius, a thrilling indictment, is what most alerted me to the depth and root of our collective crisis of spirit as it stands today, and strengthened my commitment to actions that remind all citizens, including myself, that we don't have to put on pseudo-intellectual disaffected minstrel shows to redeem ourselves or this oppressive regime, that we can relax, that our focused calm would be much more frightening than dancing on our own graves.

Fueling this semi-aimless frenzy for new footage is a collective obsession with anything that can be watched, anything that merits a reaction, anything that spikes the social adrenaline, which is to say anything that renders us passive and at the mercy of its image, affording us those amnesiac moments wherein we can hide the difference between action and reaction, call to duty and call to sophisticated and overblown clickbait or gossip that feels obligatory, like some broken spoke in the revolutionary impulse dragging its muted pride across every five-minute headline. Watching videos like the one for "This Is America," and entering the mostly insincere debates that follow, is to vigilance and true civic communion as soulful, uncompromising art is to a Pepsi commercial or a Miss America pageant, except in the less blatantly superficial context of black music or semi-radical politics it's as if we're all auditioning for best liberal in show. It's rare that the spectacle becomes something we try to protect and rescue from its own oblivion, and it's rare that the show made for pure entertainment is backed by any ideology besides exigent leisure. This era is rare, like Armageddon. Everything reeks of agenda. And our luxury, the freedom to casually and idly watch economic and political turmoil unfold and escalate, to behave as if we're removed from the interplay of the events, demigods in the machine, is the most dangerous aspect of our assimilation. In a culture that does not carry the tradition of call and response that makes West African models of performer and spectator so human and natural, so interactive, and that makes the Puritans mad at Magic Johnson Theatre loud, we all get caught in narcissistic echo chambers because all we demand of interaction is a platform. We aren't practiced in feeling one another out beyond contrived codes of etiquette; we don't improvise well with one another but we've grown skilled at faking it. The ideal American audience can be silent or pretend or guided by cue cards as long as there are bodies in the seats, followers, big numbers. The joys of simulation, simulacra, consuming images in this one-sided way are diminishing, they become the discontents of exploitation, mimicry, corporations selling our images back to us depraved and in their Sunken Place. In this way we are removed from our instinctive responses to our happily corrupt government and the okey-doke culture that mirrors it, and our idea of political participation is our abstract and grandiose obsessing over what we should sacrifice or uphold hypothetically for the big numbers in those empty seats, before we even address the mundane and the tangible, what we can hold onto of our better selves, the impact concrete daily habits, rituals, have on our ideology and likelihood to make good on claims that we seek 'change.' And if we're this addicted to outrage and to watching this collapse of empire like it's reality TV or fodder on our wings, we're unlikely to overturn it, we're too invested, the status quo is too much a part of our identities as liberals, our brand, our grand lie. We would kill for it, on video at least. Our favorite artists offer us more of the outrageous, give us more opportunities for our sanguine outrage. In this atmosphere the outcry for change becomes a false posture, a costume we can all put on and dance around in online or even in the streets with signs and face paint, but take it off just as readily and head to the mall or to Coachella or to buy some Coca-Cola and an *US Weekly*.

Willingness to be obedient spectators, to receive images instead of demanding and producing them, is a kind of spirit sickness, in my estimation, a pathology, a love of lack and a disdain for agency, and that love, unrequited, grows more and more desperate and servile and willing to overlook its object's transgressions for a little validation. I'm suggesting that we divest from this amorous frenzy, this petit-bourgeoisie echo chamber, this new American greeting card, and meditate, every day. It might not garner the glamour of western intelligentsia or that split-second attention of pop culture, to sit quietly with a blank mind, a big white or black and infrared space where cycles of thought and received ideas and images and ideological stances would revolve like body counts, to just take twenty minutes a day and shut that off, to shut up triumphantly. It might not sound as revolutionary as the gesture of voicing another opinion, it might not come with as long a cheat sheet as social media, but a clearing, a decongestion of the senses, has been for me the first step to the original and the healthy and the in-the-undercommons, ideas for what to do next, for how to remain sincere and not just reactionary, soulful and not just loud about some fast feelings, curious and not just hip, Afro-Surrealist without the need to court violence and shame to access the inherent strangeness in every encounter.

I love us, in our madness, but we all need our own private unraveling and recentering daily if we're going to survive this phase of America. We need to be the center of our own attention in a healing way, not just needy for the resonance of our own naive freedom calls. It's in that deep listening to ourselves, in our solitude, that we discover real necessary next steps, hear the collective, receive ideas about which mode of action will be productive and which is vain or vapid and ventriloquized even though it seems noble. Let us stop muting the collective listening that can happen when we tune ourselves individually first, become worthy of our own conversation, demand more for our bodies and minds and spirits than passive spectatorship and babbling opinions. From there maybe divesting from economically and environmentally toxic brands, product by product, becomes more viable, volunteering to teach or offer the arts in some capacity in underserved communities becomes a lighthearted walk through your clear mind, exercising more often, getting more sun, feeling more alive, thinking about Flint and donating water and writing about the ongoing crisis there, looking into how to help migrant families and then doing so—all of this becomes more accessible when the mind sits still away from the constant reel of images for a short while every day and explores sensations and intelligences beyond thought. Secular meditation makes it easy to remember that, beyond received interpretations of the dismal state American society is in, there are reasons to be defiantly sensual and human, to have a body, to prevail and take action, reasons that transcend all politicking and help our so-called political participation come from a place more like peace than factionalism. I want to remember what it is we are even trying to save in this next election. That's what will get us to the polls en masse. No amount of mutual angst can replace the feeling of being heard as a catalyst for action.

Before you're on the radio or in a video being big and white and not sure how you got so good at it as a black man or a black woman, or a white man or an Asian woman or an American of any disposition, check out your mind. Spectators are body snatchers, and maybe it's time we watch ourselves, steal our minds back little by little, from the barren buzzing hive of digitized action, just for a few minutes a day. Recognize that this, this body, this mind, isn't America. You don't have to represent such a stale idea, you can be new unto this land, you don't have to be tormented to be of value, you don't even have to comment if your lifestyle and daily acts prove whose side you're on and why. You don't have to be big and white to win this round.

OBFUSCATION
IS THE ENEMY

by Rick Moody

Passionate readers of Orwell know well about the destruction of language under totalitarian regimes. While *doublespeak*, *doublethink*, and *newspeak* date to *1984*, published in 1949, George Orwell was thinking about the effect of politics on language even earlier, in "Politics and the English Language" (1946). Obfuscation is the enemy in Orwell's essay, the sign of a fell purpose, and of the tendency of language to become vague in the political theater in order to mask the inhumanities of political regimes.

Our current situation, as regards usage in political speech, is so much worse than mere ambiguity or obfuscation that it renders Orwell's predictive capabilities apparently quaint.

Trump's assault on language began, on the campaign trail, with his reiterations of the bugbear of "political correctness," which I have elsewhere pointed out amounts to a rooting out of a foe that does not in a practical sense exist. Opposition to the "politically correct," like the preservation of religious liberty in a denial-of-services context, is actually pro-racist and pro-homophobic language which rhetorically finds its footing by meaning the very opposite of what it appears to mean. When "religious liberty" is uttered in a denial-of-services context, that is, what it means to do is to allow the utterer to freely prevent the liberty of others. When Donald Trump opposes "political correctness" what he is attempting to erect is a set of parameters for a "prejudicial correctness," rhetorical guidelines for racist speech that will allow it to take place under a veneer of rectitude.

The same complete reversal of manifest content is apparent in the term "fake news." This term clearly, to even the most casual viewer, signifies reporting that is verifiable but potentially damaging to the regime. To designate, for example, an entire network an "enemy of the people" is to attempt to create a climate of self-designed veracity in which language cannot render the factual without approval of the patriarchal regulatory entity. Not only does the term "fake news" damage the institutional credibility of the Fourth

Estate, not only does it devalue factual investigation, but it also infantilizes the regime's base, so that this base can tolerate only disseminatory pabulum from the regime itself.

This control of meanings, then, is very like the "freedom is slavery" model of propaganda in Orwell's *1984*. While we in the United States of the present are used to the control of the marketplace of ideas under totalitarian regimes like China's or Russia's, we are lucky enough to have avoided firsthand experience with the manipulation of signs in a totalitarian way. The breathtaking extremity of rhetorical control in the Trump era gives us a fresh experience of this absolute manipulation.

The apex of the assault on meaning and language that orbits around Donald Trump comes to be in the concept of "truthful hyperbole," which is his attempt to codify the practical application of pervasive mendacity to everyday life. This is a phrase that Orwell, in "Politics and the English Language," would have found especially illustrative. The term is patently oxymoronic, since hyperbole by its nature is an overstatement of the facts, and the polysyllabic yoking together of these opposites, *truthful* and *hyperbole*, is a purposeful attempt to lipstick the pig. (An interesting feature of "truthful hyperbole" is that Trump used it first in *The Art of the Deal*, making the book a rare example of a non-fiction work that advertises itself as fictive.)

Orwell, in illustrating the totalitarian impulse, often depicts it as incremental. A great number of steps are required to deceive an entire nation. Trump's assault on language is an opening salvo in a scaling up of dictatorial intent. Further signs of the impulse include, for instance, attempts to remove managerial personnel at the FBI in order to control the outcome of the Russia investigation.

Yes, democracy itself is at stake, and not just the meaning of the word *democracy*, which now appears to mean the opposite of what it formerly meant in the United States of America, now something closer to "the unyielding control of a large indigent population of low-wage workers by a plutocratic elite while persuading this indigent population that it needs and wants to be controlled"–not only in words, but institutionally, morally, militarily.

The key to overturning the rhetorical and moral decay of the Trump presidency is to retake the House of Representatives, thereby restoring checks and balances to the American government and the power of subpoena to the minority. Don't stay home in November.

MORE FOR MORE THAN ME

by Tracy O'Neill

As a child, I was prone to theatrics meant to corroborate my own value. An aunt owned a brown coffee tin stamped with the faces of the presidents, and I'd recite their names to prove I was intelligent enough to sit with the adults at family gatherings. When I recited prayers, I thought their declamation demonstrated that my virtue exceeded that of those who failed to memorize theirs. And when my mother permitted me to audition for dance performances, I would shimmy in front of people with clipboards, intending to perform charm sufficient to ensure my future performance of charm over the other hopefuls. I was, like most hams, attached to the cult of the individual.

Back then, I had no reservations about competitive individualism. I picked up a non-team sport and viewed its contests as equally distributed opportunities to exact willpower on empty futures. I wanted my place, whatever it took, and I did not worry about who would be excluded because I was certain inclusion was always possible, that you could net whatever you wanted through personal endeavor. In my days as a praying, tap-dancing anthropomorphic memory palace, I believed human effort limitless and limitlessly available to everyone equally, even as I accepted the position that value was tied to scarcity of resources. I did not see that neoliberalism's love affair with the laissez-faire hinged on supernatural beliefs.

But, like many children, at a certain point I had to abandon magical thinking. In various jobs I have held as an adult, I have learned, for example, that:

1. A day has an endpoint. Therefore, an infinite number of tasks cannot be fit into a workday, no matter what an employer chasing efficiency might believe.

2. Bodies require calories. Calories cost money in a capitalist society. Therefore, a baseline living wage is required to do a good or even mediocre job.

3. A dead person cannot perform. Therefore, health care provides the necessary conditions for producing value.

4. Babies are not self-sufficient. Therefore, paid
   family leave matters immensely to those interested
   in the simultaneous continuation of humanity and
   a functioning economy.

For many workers, however, persuading employers of these fundamentals proves immensely difficult. Individual grievances–and accomplishments–do not tip working conditions into reason. Abstract fantasies of efficiency, austerity, and market freedoms obscure the most basic facts about the requirements of human life. The non-biological entity of the company must be kept "alive," even at the expense of its living, breathing laborers. If the terms of employment are insufficient, employees are often told they should work more in the nonexistent additional hours of the day; make their bodies healthy enough, without medical care, to not require medical care; need less; lean in; and so on. It becomes the worker's burden to disprove that the lack of survival necessities has been precipitated by individual failings.

Organized labor, however, offers an alternative. Where the prevailing logics of neoliberalism shame individual workers for their inability to thrive under the unlivable conditions it produces, labor unions are able to bring these collective struggles into view. They open up space for solidarity rather than making rights contingent on solo spectacles of worth. And they can harness the power of the group to push for change.

The data is clear. Union workers earn more than their non-union counterparts. They pay less for benefits. There is a smaller gender wage gap for union members than for non-union laborers. And union members are more likely to have fully paid family leave.

The path to collective bargaining is not always easy, of course. When graduate student workers at Columbia University voted to unionize—and when the union was recognized by the National Labor Relations Board—the university retained legal counsel at Proskauer Rose in an attempt to break it. And in the gig economy, labor organization faces several challenges, including the fact that under the National Labor Relations Act protection for engaging in collective action is not provided to independent contractors.

But there are several ways we can support labor unions. We can start one ourselves. We can refuse to cross a picket line. We can communicate to our alma maters that we will not give to institutions that refuse to bargain with unions. We can reject politicians who aim to weaken unions. And we can push for laws that recognize the right of gig workers to organize.

We can outgrow competitive individualism. We can embrace worker solidarity. We can.

POLITICALLY CORRECT?
HEAR ME OUT, PLEASE

by CAConrad

"It is not our differences that divide us. It is our inability to recognize, accept, and celebrate those differences."

–Audre Lorde

The term "politically correct" has always bothered me because it suggests that the need to forge safe spaces in which people can live without fear is merely wallowing in the filth and conspiracy of politics. When I was outed in high school in the mid-'80s, I watched friends trade my kindness and love for them for the homophobic cruelty aimed at me by everyone else. When the heterosexual Christian town you live in brands you the Town Faggot, is it politically correct to ask for the violence to stop? When my boyfriend Earth was brutally tortured, raped, and burned alive in Tennessee, and the police refused to investigate, and the sheriff called me Faggot like it was my name and told me to mind my own business, was it politically correct of me to want justice for the man I loved?

Instead of politically correct, maybe it's just plain *correct* to love someone and want them to have a place in this world where they are not persecuted and murdered. If you are someone who uses the term "politically correct" to dismiss the needs and concerns of others, try taking a moment before you say the words and ask yourself why you need to say them at all. What does it cost you to consider keeping your mouth shut? Better yet, what would it cost you to open your mouth and ask people what they may need and what you can do to help?

If you are a registered voter in the United States, please look carefully into your state's upcoming elections for anti-LGBTQ referendums and bigoted politicians who need to be fired. Voters in Massachusetts, for instance, are complacent in their state's usually progressive political leanings, but this November will see a truly vicious referendum called the Massachusetts Gender Identity Anti-Discrimination Veto Referendum: an attempt by neo-fascists to remove a law that protects LGBTQ people from discrimination in hotels, restaurants, and other privately owned public places where heterosexuals have always been welcome. This referendum needs to be read carefully, because many liberal voters will think that voting *no* means voting against discriminatory practices–when in fact they need to vote *yes* to uphold the protections the law still provides.

Let us take this time before the elections to contact all of our friends and family across the nation and ask them to please pay close attention to these laws.

Here is some good news: business owners in Kentucky are taking their state's anti-LGBTQ legislation into their own hands before the upcoming elections. Many businesses throughout Kentucky are placing stickers on their doors that read *WE DON'T DISCRIMINATE: If you're buying, we're selling.* Remember the anti-LGBTQ legislation Vice President Pence approved as governor of Indiana? Well, high-school students are holding the first ever Pride event in his hometown of Columbus, Indiana. In more good news, voters in Michigan who are tired of Christian conversion therapy being used on young LGBTQ people are trying to pass Bill 5550, which will ban conversion therapy in their state.

The rise of ACT UP and Queer Nation was the time when we took back the word *queer*. Queer took the power back, not asking for but demanding our space in the world.

Queer was the first time I felt comrades had my back. Queer was sick and tired of the racism, misogyny, transphobia, and classism in the gay and lesbian community. Politically correct, you say? Oh no, you have it all wrong! The people who claim my community is politically correct are actually the ones doing the correct political things to make the United States a ruthless, murderous nation of intolerance.

Sasha Wall of South Carolina bravely lived the last three years of her life as a woman. Her dream, she thought, could fit into this world of dreamers. On Easter Sunday this year she was shot to death while sitting in her car at an intersection. For two hours people drove around her dead body slumped over the steering wheel until someone finally checked to see if she needed help. African American transwomen have one of the highest rates of murder in the United States. If it has not been apparent before, I hope it is finally becoming clear that LGBTQ organizations have spent too much time and too many resources on "marriage equality" and supporting a racist military-industrial complex while the most vulnerable members of our community go without proper care for their health and safety. BLACK TRANS LIVES MATTER!

According to the *Los Angeles Blade*, more than 70 percent of the 2017 spike in violence against LGBTQ people in the United States was against queer people of color.

Yet many conservative minds today, like Jordan Peterson, are busy whining that political correctness is a form of mind control instead of asking why it is people need to demand space to speak, space to actually exist without being shot to death in their cars. Does Peterson, wealthy, white, heterosexual man that he is, think Sasha Wall was politically correct in her quest to live her dream, the quest that cost her her life?

Yes, I am queer, but even if you are not, my community is still your community just as much as your community is mine. It is time to finally get rid of all and any lawmakers who terrorize LGBTQ people. Be careful with Democrats who are too eager to reach across party lines. Georgia, Kansas, and Oklahoma have upcoming adoption laws "protecting" Christian adoption agencies from LGBTQ parents.

Subcomandante Marcos said, "In our dreams we have seen another world, an honest world, a world decidedly more fair than the one in which we now live." In saying this he was telling us we share this dream, one we must admit is our bond, and now we must manifest it, build it, walk directly into that future we dream together. The price of not believing we can make this other, better world is living in the same old world of inequity we feel tearing our bodies apart. What is stopping our faith in one another is merely a handful of people. When we consider the fact that three million more popular votes went to Hillary Clinton, it is easy to see that the majority has a different kind of dream than Trump's much smaller neo-fascist constituency. With the weight of three million more humans, let the dream-manifesting begin!

As grim as things are, we really are standing together on a political hinge. Let's force the right and the right-leaning left as far left as possible. Let's not settle for more neoliberal candidates as Democrats any more than we settle for Republicans of any kind. Let's use this opportunity we have today to tip our nation in the direction of an America worthy of the principles the politicians are so busy bragging about. Be well and let's work together!

THE HUNDRED PERCENT DOCTRINE

by Karen Joy Fowler

I commit to take action because Trump has no plan to keep us safe in a time of hurricanes, floods, droughts, wildfires, and extinctions. By us, I mean all of us–people, plants, fellow creatures, this land that belongs to you and me.

Back in the Pleistocene, when the war on terror was being sold to the American public, Dick Cheney said this: "If there's a 1 percent chance that Pakistani scientists are helping al Qaeda build or develop a nuclear weapon, we have to treat it as a certainty in terms of our response." The stakes, a grave threat to life on earth, were too dire to do otherwise. This position came to be known as the One Percent Doctrine.

Today we might dub Trump's response to climate change the Hundred Percent Doctrine. If you can find even one scientist who thinks climate change doesn't pose a grave threat to life on earth, then you're free to ignore the issue completely.

Did I say ignore? I meant exacerbate. Trump's climate policy to date includes maximizing fossil fuel extraction and usage. He boasts of reducing environmental regulations and of withdrawing from international cooperation. He wants to mine uranium in the Grand Canyon, drill for oil off our coasts. He wants to bring back coal and reduce solar and wind energy. One of his first actions in office was to green-light the Keystone XL pipeline. By March he'd slashed federal funding for climate-change research. By August, the Department of Agriculture had actually forbidden the use of the words *climate change* themselves.

Only the military continues to plan for the catastrophe that 97 percent of scientists believe is coming, and those military plans are for adaptation, not avoidance. This is not an arena in which a military win is possible, not in the long run. So we have to ask ourselves: are generals and soldiers the people we want dealing with this issue? Are they the best equipped to save and manage diminishing resources?

We get this wrong and everybody dies.

The United States is an idea and a people, but also, importantly, a place. Trump is profoundly indifferent to the wealth we share—our beautiful parks, our coastlines, our fruited plains, and the aquifers over and into which the pipelines are already leaking. Laws to prevent the pollution of our air and water are being hastily repealed. In a reversal of fifty years of policy, industries can now kill migrating birds. Wolf pups can be shot in their dens, bears as they hibernate.

If Trump can't put a thing in his bank account, it has no value to him. In fact, he appears to delight in its destruction. This spiritual void, in and of itself, should be disqualifying in a leader. His ignorance of and, more importantly, his uninterest in the challenges of climate change are definitely disqualifying.

Make America Great Again is a plan to look for the future in the past. It won't be found there. No leader can remain ignorant of the ways the world is changing and also usher us safely onward. It's our misfortune to live in a time where the future is unspeakably fragile, but the misfortune will fall most tragically on the generations to come. Trump is not the president we, and they, so desperately need.

A FEW WORDS IN DEFENSE
OF AMERICAN INSTITUTIONS
(WHICH IS TO SAY, US)

by Martin Seay

I commit to vote because the Trump presidency constitutes an unprecedented challenge to American institutions.

We hear this phrase often, or some variation of it: assault on, disruption of, challenge to American institutions. It's worth being specific about what this means. American institutions include all the branches and functions of government—federal, state, and local—but also the market economy, the free and independent press, and a host of civil, religious, scientific, medical, educational, and cultural organizations, as well as an array of venues and platforms for sports, arts, and entertainment, all of which interact to produce the quotidian texture of life in the United States.

To a greater or lesser extent, every last one of these has been unsettled by the election of Donald J. Trump.

We should also be clear that not every institution merits safeguarding, and not every institutional disruption ought to be condemned. Prior to the Civil War, for instance, white Southerners referred to slavery euphemistically but not inaccurately as a "peculiar institution," and in the years since emancipation an entrenched system of laws and practices has maintained racial inequality by limiting African Americans' access to employment, credit, education, and justice. Though we portray ourselves as a nation of pioneers and immigrants, throughout much of our history our actual policy toward new arrivals has been bigoted and exclusionary, while our treatment of the continent's earliest inhabitants has ranged from resentful to genocidal. Formally denied suffrage until 1920, women remain subject to deep-rooted assumptions and expectations that prevent their equal participation in every aspect of the American experience. Powerful and persistent institutional forces perpetuate each of these instances of unfairness, and should rightly be opposed.

What's different about Trump's challenge to American institutions—what earns it the status of existential threat and national emergency—is that the institutions it targets are the fundamental principles set forth in our founding documents: the rule of law that safeguards our individual freedoms, and the democratic system through which we assert our pluralistic interests. However imperfect they may be in their application and results, these remain our best means of reconciling our differences and advancing our common welfare.

Whether these fundamental institutions will successfully defend themselves and hold the current administration to account for its abuses remains to be seen. The most insidious damage inflicted by these assaults will probably also be the most enduring. Human behavior is shaped less by values than by norms; the unavoidable lag between capricious violations of the basic tenets of responsible governance and the legal and political redress of those violations engenders a creeping expectation that this conduct is tolerable. Tolerated long enough, it begins to seem normal.

What many have long cautioned is now painfully clear: many Americans simply do not value the fundamental institutions that Trump and his allies have targeted. Instead, they evince a blithe willingness–even a perfervid eagerness–to see these institutions warped and adulterated in the interest of maintaining a familiar social hierarchy, one that's solidly patriarchal and white-supremacist. To these Americans, the preservation of this social order is worth surrendering their own freedom from corporate predation, their access to affordable health care, and their expectation that public officials serve without corruption. These voters have been a force in our politics throughout the history of the republic, one that responded to the eight years of the Obama presidency with particularly convulsive force, and that is now conspicuously untroubled by their chosen president's chumminess with the ascendant authoritarians of other nations. These people aren't going anywhere, and they aren't going to change their minds.

Most Americans, however, remain profoundly invested in the endurance of our fundamental institutions, and must now commit to energetically asserting that investment on Election Day. Further, we must commit to testifying, however we are able, to the fact that the behavior of this president and his administration is neither normal nor acceptable, and cannot begin to be perceived as such. Finally, we must work to ensure that these fundamental institutions exercise their legitimate authority to undo the reactionary forces that contradict them, to take the present disaster as an occasion to reconcile our practices with our values. In order to survive, freedom and fairness must expand.

American political consciousness is undergirded by a few instances of rhetoric that almost every schoolchild can call to mind. Abraham Lincoln's assertion in his Gettysburg address of human equality as a national defining proposition, Emma Lazarus's portrayal of America as a welcoming golden door, Franklin Roosevelt's inclusion of want and fear in his list of conditions from which all people ought to be free, Martin Luther King, Jr.'s characterization of our founding documents as a promissory note–these engage the moral imagination of our citizens because they implicitly indicate that the United States is not making good on its promises, while assuring us that it can and must do so. "America never was America to me," Langston Hughes wrote in 1935, "And yet I swear this oath–America will be!"

Whatever their ultimate manifestation, all institutions arise as expressions of aggregate human will. At their worst, they become mechanisms for consolidating power and avoiding responsibility; at their best, they vastly multiply our capacity to do good. As we prepare to rescue our nation from its present peril, we do well to remember that all American institutions, whether salutary or corrupt, are the expression of a single underlying force: the huge, diverse, harried, conflicted population of individual persons that constitutes the United States, and which circumstances now call to action.

NEVER FORGET, NEVER REMEMBER

by Yahia Lababidi

I look at the lengthening shadow of violence and intolerance spreading across the Middle East, Europe, and now the Divided States of America, and I wonder if the dangerous clown that is Donald Trump might not be the moral crisis we need to awaken us both to the world's suffering and to our interconnectedness.

How is it that we are told to Never Forget 9/11 and the nearly three thousand lives taken, yet in the same breath we Never Remember the unjust "war" exacted in retribution and the hundreds of thousands of blameless, faceless Iraqi fatalities? There is no exchange rate for human suffering. All human life is sacred, all murder unholy.

Maybe we ask ourselves where Aleppo is and why we should care. We find ourselves confronted at home with gun violence, police brutality, the open wound of race relations, or the plaintive cry—as old as the creation of a nation—of indigenous Americans at Standing Rock. Or physically and psychologically damaged war veterans, homelessness, uprootedness, refugees, ISIS—all terrorists in the shape of our shadows, all side effects of the pandemic of indifference.

A prescription for our current malaise and how we might begin to heal can be found in these words by American psychiatrist M. Scott Peck:

> How strange that we should ordinarily feel compelled to hide our wounds when we are all wounded! Community requires the ability to expose our wounds and weaknesses to our fellow creatures. It also requires the ability to be affected by the wounds of others... But even more important is the love that arises among us when we share, both ways, our woundedness.

We forgive to live. As an Arab-American bridge of a man named Gibran reminds us: "Hate is a dead thing. Who of you would be a tomb?" This bears repeating during a time of Islamophobic panic, when the thirteenth-century mystic Jālāl ad-Dīn Muhammad Rūmī is a best-selling poet in America. Rūmī was a Muslim and a refugee who lived in a turbulent time not too dissimilar to our own.

What glimmer of light, what lesson might we glean from this mysterious coincidence? How is it that we readily accept that we are governed by physical laws yet believe we can afford to turn our backs on age-old spiritual laws—love, compassion, sacrifice, mercy, trust—without paying too high a price? The price of a new chance to move past the murderous folly in the Middle East and the self-defeating arrogance of the United States is nothing less than surrender of our old, failed, broken ways.

Perhaps President Trump will unwittingly Make America Great Again by bringing about a reassessment of our values. The peaceful, powerful Women's March on Washington, dwarfing the attendance of Trump's inauguration and echoing throughout the world, suggests that it might be safe to hope for change again. Provoked by his administration's disregard for science and denial of climate change, we witnessed the Scientists' March. It has been heartening, too, to witness impassioned rallies in airports throughout the country, welcoming immigrants and protesting Trump's unconstitutional executive order or "Muslim ban."

For my part, as immigrant and writer, and as a dual citizen of the U.S. and Egypt, I think of my art as a sort of peace offering. Living in America at a moment of mounting mistrust and murderous ignorance directed towards immigrants and more specifically the "Arab/Muslim world," I see all too clearly how culturally diminished and spiritually impoverished we become when we close our doors to the world and our hearts to others.

I feel a personal responsibility to serve as witness, to protest, and to address our shared humanity. So I try to communicate through my work the great peace and beauty to be found in Sufism, the mystical branch of a little understood, much-maligned faith: Islam. As Juan Ramón Jiménez says, "Ah, to be one of them! One of the poets whose song helps close the wound rather than open it!"

I REFUSE

by Sally Wen Mao

This year I am living in a historic house on the campus of George Washington University, four blocks away from the White House. Days ago, Trump's cavalcade landed on the White House lawn as he returned from a twelve-day trip to Asia, where he sat with other heads of state and mocked Kim Jong-Un in a tweet as "short and fat." I am tired. I am weary. I do not think this is funny. It is unclear whether Donald Trump knows that his xenophobic policies have already been practiced in the past, in the Geary Act that targeted Chinese immigrants and barred them from coming to this country. Those exclusion laws were also passed due to economic anxiety and a growing readiness to blame outsiders for economic strife. Needless to say, the Chinese Exclusion Acts did not help the American economy, did not lead to better lives for the disenfranchised white community. The egregious Muslim immigration bans are only a shameful repetition of history–the Trump camp has expressly stated that its policies (such as a Muslim registry) are modeled after Japanese internment camps.

Trump has fueled and encouraged racial discrimination and unrest, willfully, with impunity. He has encouraged his supporters to harass and assault protesters–often people of color–at his own rallies. Immediately following Donald Trump's election, I noticed a surge in discriminatory acts and hate crimes: not just in the news, but against my friends, their families, ordinary Americans on my Facebook feed. Donald Trump supports and validates racists, and has made it okay for them to parade their bigotry in the streets without hoods, chanting on what they feel is rightfully theirs. Charlottesville or New York, it's happening all around us. A man harassed me at a diner in the East Village, telling me to "go back to Tokyo" after complaining about how the *Hamilton* cast had disrespected Mike Pence, then pepper-sprayed a Latino man who defended me. One of my friends was called Chink as she was walking down the street. Another was pushed in the subway. Another was spat on. It is not safe to be a person of color in America. The virulent anti-immigrant and anti-people-of-color atmosphere, the desire to regress to a whites-only state, is no longer a latent feeling–it is an onslaught that will build up, every day, until we are paralyzed. But I refuse. I refuse refuse refuse refuse refuse to accept this reality, to accept this administration's brazen allegiance to bigotry.

WHY I'LL KEEP PROTESTING
by Kevin Boyle

I promise to keep protesting because of Abby and Nan.

They'd both phoned late on election night, Nan from college, Abby from a watch party gone wrong. Our lovely daughters, crying for their country.

I don't remember what I said to them. Something meant to be comforting, no doubt. But how do you comfort true believers when the principles they thought to be inviolate have suddenly been broken? How do you tell them to keep the faith?

It turns out I didn't have to. When Donald Trump was elected Abby was a year into her first job after graduation, doing social-media work for a progressive organization everyone thought would close up shop once Hillary was inaugurated. After the vote, donations surged. The organization added staff. And Abby settled in.

Through all the provocations of President Trump's first year—his assaults on immigrants and refugees, his repeated race-baiting, his defense of Klansmen, his constant attacks on the press, his reckless talk of nuclear war—she sat with her laptop, coding thoughtful, impassioned, idealistic appeals in support of the policies the new administration wanted to dismantle. Compared to the president's outrages, her messages barely registered. But on the night John McCain voted against the Obamacare repeal Abby called me again. This time she wasn't crying.

Right around then Nan started her first job.

She'd been offered a Peace Corps posting in Malawi a month before the election. We sent her off in June 2017, a whippet-thin twenty-two-year-old trudging down the concourse on her way to one of the poorest places on earth. After a summer's training, she was assigned to teach English in a rural school. Her fellow teachers gave her a house with a garden, two classes overflowing with students, and the sort of welcome you hope your child will get eight thousand miles from home.

In the Malawian countryside American news arrives in fits and starts. But when the president dismissed all of Africa with an adolescent slur of unmistakably racist intent, Nan heard. She called a couple of days later. His cruelty had really bothered her. But she didn't have time to dwell on it, not when she was trying to get a room full of teenagers to write a few sentences about a short story they'd read and to corral the little kids who crowd onto her porch every afternoon to draw with the colored pencils she has to share. Not when she had work to do.

That's why I joined the Women's March, the protests against the Muslim Ban, the rallies against the racist violence in Charlottesville, and the March for Our Lives, and why I'll keep protesting, though the truth is I'd prefer to stay home. Because our courageous daughters have refused to surrender their nation to the hatred our president embraces, because in their quiet ways they've stood for the principles he betrays, because they still believe. I can't come close to matching their dedication. But I am honored to stand with them.

XENOPHOBIA, BIGOTRY, AND HATRED

by Mitra Jouhari

I commit to take action because every day that Trump holds office is another day I spend wondering when I'll get to see my family again.

I am Iranian-American, first generation, which is a hard thing to be right now.

Targeted discrimination towards Middle Eastern countries is nothing new. It was happening before Trump and will continue after his reign comes to its welcome end. However, the intensity with which this administration has sought to discriminate against people from predominantly Muslim countries is new. The energy that Trump devotes to trying to shove Muslim bans through the legal system terrifies me. My family is in Iran. When will they be able to come visit? When will I see my grandpa again? Why must their travel be limited because of the actions of a select few?

I know the answer. Xenophobia, bigotry, and hatred.

As I write this, John Bolton is set to start his work as National Security Advisor in a matter of days. Time and time again, he has advocated for war with Iran. His bigotry finds a welcome home in the Trump administration and with those who empower it. I fear what he will be able to accomplish, the damage he will do along the way. I fear losing my family.

I commit to take action because I am tired of living in this state of constant terror. I am tired of hearing politicians make baseless claims about people living in countries they know nothing about and, at least in Trump's case, probably couldn't even find on a map. I want to do all I can to strip power from the people who elevate, spread, and embody toxic rhetoric and ideologies.

I commit to take action because I believe my love for my family is stronger than the hatred Trump has for people who look like me.

THERE IS NO END TO THAT SEASON ANYMORE

by Bill McKibben

I commit to take action because one country has poured more carbon dioxide into the earth's atmosphere than any other. That country is the United States–and thanks to Donald Trump it is also the one country that is not willing to join with the rest of the world to try and solve our gravest crisis.

Think about that. Every other nation on earth–even Syria, which barely has a functioning central government–has signed on to the Paris Accords. We signed on, too, of course, but then Donald Trump signed us off. His reasoning made little sense: somehow he decided it was a "bad deal" for the U.S., even though it asked very little of us, and even though we had–this bears repeating–caused most of the problem. You want to know whom global warming is a bad deal for? Bangladesh. The Maldives. Fiji. They caused none of the problem–their carbon emissions are a rounding error in any global table–and they are going to lose huge chunks of their territory. The Marshall Islands? They may sink.

But we'll take at least some of the punishment, too. Indeed, as if guided by karma, the months after Trump's grandstand play have featured America's worst rainstorm (fifty-one inches in Hurricane Harvey), the world's longest stretch of 185 mile-per-hour winds (Irma) and the utter ugly destruction that María brought to Puerto Rico. Napa and Sonoma–the good life defined–saw a fire that took forty-two lives follow hard on the heels of record heat and drought. It was barely put out when Santa Barbara and environs caught fire–the largest blaze in California history, which came in December, two months after the traditional end of the state's wildfire season. But there is no end to that season anymore, not in our hot dry new world. And no end to the troubles: after the fire finished burning all the plants in the area, epic rains produced mudslides that killed twenty people. The U.S. set a new record for costliest disasters last year.

In that kind of world, it's a constant and ongoing menace to have as president a man who believes climate change is a hoax invented by the Chinese. Everyone's entitled to disagree about policy, but disagreeing about physics is something that neither our nation nor our world can, at this late date, afford.

IT POURS DOWN

by Raquel Salas Rivera

The image of Donald Trump tossing paper towels into a crowd of Puerto Ricans is cemented in the public imaginary of the United States as a disrespectful moment, but few people in the mainland U.S. know that much of the audience for that visit was made up of folks who had been living in nearby shelters. One morning, they were rounded up, put on buses, and taken to visit Trump. Those most in need were chosen for this humiliation. Behind each new news scandal, there are people who are being exterminated or whose lives are being destroyed.

Puerto Rico has long been a testing ground for imperialist policies, from the forced sterilization that began when Law 116 was established in 1936–which resulted in the sterilization of approximately one-third of all Puerto Rican women of childbearing age–to the Navy's occupation of its sister island Vieques, where it performed routine military tests for decades. The Puerto Rican people have been exploited and used as guinea pigs since 1898. The newest chapter in this history of colonial experimentation has included the implementation of the PROMESA bill, the forced restructuring of Puerto Rico, and the subsequent infrastructural abandonment on the part of federal governmental agencies such as the Federal Emergency Management Agency (FEMA).

Trump united white supremacists under a pirate flag and gave them permission to raid Caribbean islands. My Puerto Rico is under siege. El Morro, the old Spanish fort, now stands as a remnant, reminding tourists that Spain once ran things, but behind this museum is the real fort: the Jones Act, an invisible economic wall that keeps out the resources we need the most. Established as part of the Merchant Marine Act of 1920, this law gives the U.S. complete monopoly over which ships can enter or leave Puerto Rican ports. Immediately after Hurricane María hit the island, the Jones Act limited the aid that could arrive by limiting the entry of ships from countries other than the United States. Households were left without enough food or clean water, left to depend on help from FEMA, which either showed up with boxes full of junk food or never arrived.

Trump and the interests he represents hope to push Puerto Ricans off the island so they can use their companies to rebuild a Puerto Rico in their image–a Puerto Rico without Puerto Ricans—where basic services are inaccessible and everything, from education to health care, has a price. This post-María abandonment has a purpose: to force those living here into destitution and lower property values so vulture capitalists can buy cheap land and build more hotels and casinos. If he can do it in Puerto Rico, he can do it anywhere, making us once more a preferred experimental location.

This is why many Puerto Ricans were forced to leave the island in the hopes that they would find better living conditions in the U.S. mainland. Since the hurricane, approximately two thousand Boricuas moved to Philadelphia, but things aren't necessarily better here. On February 14, FEMA began withdrawing support for Puerto Rican families displaced by the aftereffects of Hurricane María and currently living in Philadelphia, leaving them homeless. Many of these Boricuas have had difficulty acquiring work because they do not speak English. What will happen to them? They are unable to go back, unable to stay, and stuck in a place where they are treated like second-class citizens by racists who don't know and don't care. Newly arrived Boricuas learn that hate doesn't trickle down, it pours down. There is no protection or support in a world led by fascists who are being goaded daily by el Generalíssimo Trump. Fascism isn't new, but each new manifestation of fascism under this regime means more of my people are killed or left for dead.

In the U.S. mainland, there has been talk of impeachment, but if Trump were impeached, would he get to live out his days in his wealthy home? Where is justice? Behind notions such as *embarrassment*, *shame*, and *nation*, there is murder, destitution, and colonialism. It is necessary to think beyond the supposedly reparative gesture of the public scolding. Trump isn't white America's bumbling racist uncle. He is a war criminal, a mass murderer, the world's Darth Vader. He runs an empire.

In order to end this tyrannical reign, we must be able to imagine a world without colonialism, without Trump, without the International Monetary Fund or the World Bank. Let's imagine a world where Puerto Rico can be truly free; where my people can expect more than food, clean water, and a roof; a world where we can live where we want (including Puerto Rico) and where we can go to the ocean and not fear a wave of new colonizers who show up wearing khakis and red caps and carrying bills that say we aren't *fit* to rule ourselves. In this new world, we will be worth more than a falsified debt and all our poems will flood the streets, forcing the old waters to recede.

Repeal the Jones Act!
Cancel the debt!
Decolonize Puerto Rico!

BE COUNTED
by Jim Shepard

One of the immediate challenges facing any sentient American when confronting what our current president has done in his first year in office is how to combat overload when it comes to sorting through the various forms and targets of his destructiveness. And one way of doing that is to ask which of the changes he has wrought will be most difficult to undo once he is finally returned to the status he merits. His tax policies, for all their unjust heartlessness, stand a good chance of being rolled back, for example, as do most if not all of his pillage-the-earth environmental policies. His impact on our judiciary system, on the other hand, is much more lasting, given our lack of recourse when it comes to horrible appointments; this last year, unhappily, set a record for the most appellate judges confirmed in a president's first year in office.

But for me it's the drastic acceleration of the country's slide into authoritarianism that's the most concerning and potentially irreversible. For forty years now the Republican party has profited from a pernicious feedback loop: generating hostility in Americans toward their own government by claiming government doesn't work, then seeming to prove their point once in power. That, combined with the opposition party's own corruption and fecklessness, has persuaded a lot of Americans that representative democracy is a hopeless logjam and that they are therefore justified in turning away from civic life, becoming consumers rather than citizens. But our current President's initiatives are so transparent in their radical self-interest that huge majorities of Americans are recognizing that their government is actively pursuing agendas they deplore. Which leaves, principally, two alternatives. One is the distracted and irritated sense that someone *should do something*–that someone *not* being the citizen–the result being support for the ascension of a figure who cuts through the Gordian knot and gets the trains to run on time and promises to protect us from bogeymen. The other is an understanding that the system is not going to fix itself and that if that system is the problem we can overwhelm it from below through our energy and commitment.

The bad news about that first alternative is that American society is now so profoundly tilted to the right that in many ways the stage for authoritarianism is already set. One party has figured out how to paralyze our legislative branch, and the other refuses to learn how to combat that strategy; the judiciary has over the last few decades been stuffed with conservative ideologues; our executive branch has continually gathered power unto itself, unchecked; it's possible that our very voting system is compromised and ripe for manipulation; and the media is now so balkanized that Americans no longer share the same basic information or view of the world, on top of which it is dominated by a right-wing network dedicated to promoting *dis*information. Maybe even more importantly, this new administration has normalized the notion that it's okay for our leaders to blithely and repeatedly lie to us, and we might be about to pass our biggest Rubicon yet, in terms of our commitment to honoring the rule of law, should it transpire that our president broke the law and our Congress decides it doesn't care.

One of the most telling indicators of where Weimar Germany was headed, according to most historians who study it, was the disparity in the state's treatment of violence depending upon its origins: violence perpetrated by the left was brutally punished, while violence initiated by the right occasioned a slap on the wrist. If that sounds familiar, well, that's why I brought it up.

The good news is that the democratic impulse is way more powerful in America in 2018 than it was in Germany in 1930, and there's evidence everywhere that Americans are ready to take representative democracy into their own hands. For example, confronting an administration openly contemptuous of many issues they support, a record number of women are running for office for the first time: nearly four hundred so far are planning to run for the House of Representatives, the highest number in history. These are citizens standing up to be counted from all parts of the nation, willing to engage the hard work involved to bring their ideas to the table and do their bit for the collective good, just as the Founding Fathers envisioned. So while there are good reasons for Americans to feel shame and apprehension when confronting their current political situation, there are also hundreds–thousands–even millions–of additional reasons to feel pride, and hope.

THE EXTRAORDINARY SELF
by Melissa Chadburn

The afternoon of Wednesday, November 9, 2016, the first day of having Donald Trump as our president-elect, I met with a Guatemalan immigrant I'll call Sandra Henriquez. Although Henriquez couldn't vote, because she is undocumented, she had traveled to Nevada, a battleground state, to get the vote out, and she feared, like I did, the kind of world to which we had just woken up. To understand Henriquez's political commitment, you must understand her story, which is a story of rape.

Henriquez used to work as a night janitor in an office building in downtown Los Angeles. Her supervisor had told her and the other women janitors, mostly undocumented immigrants like her, that he had strong ties to a notorious gang in Guatemala and would go after their families if the women did not comply with whatever it was he wanted.

For Henriquez, things began with a leer, then progressed to the supervisor following her around at work, asking inappropriate questions, making phone calls during off hours, sending sexts. This is stuff Henriquez had no language for. Sexual harassment doesn't exist where she is from. There is rape, and no rape. All the comments, sneaky eyes, dirty feelings, and waiting-for-the-other-shoe-to-drop moments were legal in the United States, as far as she knew.

The supervisor withheld the women's paychecks unless they went with him to a hotel room. One day it was Henriquez's turn. The supervisor raped her. She became pregnant. She changed, but not in a way anyone could see. There was a deep splintering in her heart, a splintering in her actions and her beliefs. Despite the better life she was working so hard to provide for her future family in this country, she had an abortion.

Henriquez is just one of many undocumented women who are coming forward and telling their stories about being sexually harassed and assaulted in the workplace. We were meeting the morning after the election because she wanted the dangers facing the women who dust the photos on our desks at work, who refill the toilet-paper rolls in our gym restrooms, who clean the floors of our hospitals, to be known and told. These dangers now seemed even greater given what Trump's election had already unleashed in the previous few hours.

While Henriquez spoke, I watched her ordinary self turn into an extraordinary self. I heard about her suing her employer. I heard about her getting a U visa, which provides sanctuary to victims of violent crimes. I heard about her joining the *promotoras*, a group of women in east Los Angeles who host healing circles to talk to each other about sexual assault and learn about their rights in the workplace. Recently they've started something new and innovative, which ought not be so innovative: a *compañeros* circle, a place for Latino men to come and heal, and learn about what constitutes sexual harassment.

Henriquez's stories rescued me from my own solipsistic post-election despair.

She had a little baby in her arms, thrashing beside her neck, then cooing, then sleeping peacefully. Two months earlier, Henriquez and the other *promotoras* had fasted at the state capitol for a week. They were hoping Governor Brown would sign AB1978, a bill that would offer janitors more protections against sexual assault. The final day of the fast, Governor Brown signed the bill. Henriquez told me how she and the other women, all of whom were undocumented, all of whom were working in low-wage industries, and had been sexually harassed or even raped, held one another, crying in amazement over what they had been able to accomplish when they joined together.

But there was still more work to be done. Henriquez pointed out: "Someone who sexually harasses women and makes a profit off of my poor working conditions is now in office." Still the *promotoras* march, the *promotoras* heal, the *promotoras* talk, the *promotoras* dance, and they are powerful in effecting change. And yet sometimes at night Henriquez feels a piece of herself floating outside her body. The piece of her she had to let go of.

I will forever remember a time of being powerless. I remember being beaten, literally beaten, by my mother, a woman who subscribed to corporal punishment. I remember standing on one leg and reciting ridiculous rote statements to please her. I remember the little red ball of HOT in the room that she and I were both after—my surrender to her overwhelming power. I had many mantras at that time, but the one I remember most vividly is *Iwillnotbreak. Iwillnotbreak. Iwillnotbreak.*

This mantra has served me well when sitting across the table from businessmen, when negotiating union contracts, when people beside me were fighting for their lives, for their pensions, for their health care, for back pay, for basic human dignities. I have had the most power when I have rolled up my sleeves and conveyed the message: *Let's go. I've got all the time in the world. And I will not break.* While I've witnessed a similar technique employed by white guys in suits, people with personal assistants and power, people who are largely assholes, it's we who have lost everything who can do it better, because we know what it feels like to be truly powerless, to have absolutely nothing to lose. Just last week I followed a man to his apartment to get him to pay a woman for her work, and he knew he had to write that check for the sad simple fact that I had nothing else to do that night.

All around me, there are people who know how that feels. The experiences of people who are chronically homeless and children whispering goodbye to their life plans could send me deep into Twinkies and television, hot cocoa or a carafe of wine–but strangely they've done the opposite. They stoke the anger. We are not free unless those who are most marginalized are free.

Right after Trump was elected, in the moderately quiet suburb of Studio City, a man ran out of his car, bashed his hand on the ground until he broke those delicate bones, and then pulled his eye out of his head. He literally pulled his eye right out of its socket! I later learned that he'd hit a car and was probably high on PCP, but when I heard this story I thought: *Hell yeah, I wanna pull my eyes out, and I wanna light stuff on fire, and I wanna break stuff, or get my bones pummeled*. But I know my real power is in doing the unsexy work: rolling up my shirtsleeves, manning the phone banks, mobilizing, educating, building coalitions outside my usual networks, voting and getting out the vote, voting and getting out the vote, voting again.

In that small office with Henriquez, a door across the hall shut, and she quaked at the sound. At every ringing phone, every shadow, she sent a frightened glance my way. Yet the little baby in her arms helped propel her forward. This was why she had registered voters in Las Vegas when she could not vote herself; this was how she had fasted in our state capitol.

What if it were your child, your mother, your father, your sibling, who was going to be torn from you? If you had seen The Man—some officer, some uniformed person—and heard that Orders had been made, and you had only a few months to make good on your promise to keep your family intact, how fast could you walk? How soon could you knock on doors? How many conversations could you have with friends and neighbors with the little cooing baby in your arms, the small hands grasping at your chest? You would not break. That wail a baby makes when she is thrust into the bleak state of need, drumming at your neck. We are the ones we've been waiting for.

NOT HIM BUT US

by Steve Erickson

The action to which we must finally commit ourselves can't simply be about a man or president, or a political party or perhaps even a country, but about the nature of freedom and maybe nothing less than the nature of truth.

Whereas over the course of history we've had presidents who, good or bad, nonetheless saw themselves in the context of their country, now we have a president who sees the country in the context of himself. The question isn't whether he's unfit for office, which he himself has established beyond anything that anyone else can say, but whether the rest of us are fit to be Americans. This president didn't happen *to* America; *we* happened to America. In the last election we decided to believe everything terrible we had heard about his opponent and to disregard everything terrible we knew about him, and having made such a choice says something terrible about us.

There's nothing we know about him now that we didn't know before. Whether or not we voted for him for explicitly racist or sexist reasons, at the least we chose to set aside the racism and sexism in which he traffics as sufficient reasons for voting against him. In a country where, 150 years after the fact, millions won't admit that the Civil War was about slavery–the American version of Holocaust denial–we chose to set aside his baseless accusation that the first African American president wasn't a real American and wasn't a real president, an overtly racist contention that no one has ever made about a white president. We set aside innumerable toxic comments about people of other ethnicities, cultures, religions, genders; we set aside open mockery and mimicry of the physically challenged; we set aside a four-decade personal history of exploiting the poor and dispossessed; we ignored his clear authoritarian impulses and his expressed disdain for the things that constitute democracy; we shrugged off the enthusiastic endorsement of him by the Ku Klux Klan as though it meant nothing; we overlooked the cracked moral compass that can't or won't distinguish between white supremacists in Charlottesville and the woman they ran over with a car. On the world stage America is now the fat, rich old man who pushes little countries out of the way to get to the front of the photo op, straightening his tie as he does.

I was raised a Republican all those many years ago when I woke as a boy to the singing of pterodactyls outside my window, and I've been a registered independent all my voting life. Over time I've come to a prevailing suspicion of ideology both right and left that presupposes conclusions before they've been reasoned. Beyond such matters of right and left, this president didn't beget his political party in its current incarnation; his political party, cofounded a century and a half ago by the greatest American and now the most morally bankrupt political movement of our lifetime, begat him. Beyond policies that target society's most forsaken, something is rotten–I use the word in its most classic and exquisite sense–in this political party and in its national embodiment, who was born to a wealth and privilege few of us will know and who views the powerless as "losers" while whining about how unfair the world is to him. This president didn't dishonor us with his election; we dishonored ourselves. For the sake of the country we love, we need to redeem our honor while there's still time.

If the action to which we must ultimately commit ourselves can't simply be about a president, if what's gone wrong with the country won't suddenly be made right with his exit, if our new cold civil war won't be resolved by an ideology but by a vision that was supposed to resolve the last civil war, nonetheless we must begin with the prosaic. Neither investigations nor calls for impeachment will matter without wresting our government's legislative branch this November from the controlling party that cowers before its reigning despot. This will be done not by casting utopian votes for unblemished protest candidates that allow us to congratulate ourselves on our political purity; it will be done only by voting for every Democrat in sight, however much we grouse about how compromised the Democratic Party may be or about how dastardly it has been to cranky senators from Vermont.

I've lived through twelve presidents before this one and have vivid memories of ten. Sooner or later each did something to anger or frustrate or embarrass me in a manner passing (dallying with interns) or profound (laying wreaths at the graves of SS soldiers). None, however, made me ashamed of my country for having elected him—until now. We're left to resolve not who he is; we know who he is. We're left to resolve who we are, and whether we still see ourselves in the context of our country, or see the country only in the context of our worst selves, wherein no America exists at all.

I COMMIT

by Matthew Zapruder

I commit to vote because
I'm pretty sure I grab
whatever I need from the world
and place it in my mind
which is getting incrementally
like the commons
undeniably more toxic and sad
yes I too walk around
considering my intractable problems
complaining it's too late
for more sonatas
everything is already too beautiful
music and anger won't save us
yet I commit to talking

earnestly with my wife
about the school board
it will be night and we will be sitting
shoulder to shoulder
at the old table we love
each holding a pencil
like grade school children left alone at last
then in the morning
before my son wakes
I commit to holding
this tiny bit of quicksilver
(quick in the sense of living
in its very molecular nature
it wants to usefully combine with yours)
in my palm and to walking
up to the blue mailbox
I pass most mornings
in that familiar silence
under those nameless little trees
when all things that surround me wait

Dodie Bellamy is a novelist, poet, and essayist. Her most recent book is *When the Sick Rule the World*.

Tom Bissell is the author of nine books, including *Apostle*, *Magic Hours*, and (with Greg Sestero) *The Disaster Artist*.

Kevin Boyle teaches American history at Northwestern University and is the winner of the National Book Award for his 2004 book *Arc of Justice: A Saga of Race, Civil Rights, and Murder in the Jazz Age*.

Melissa Chadburn is a critic, fiction writer, and social arsonist. She is contributing editor for the Economic Hardship Reporting Project and *DAME* magazine. Her first novel, *A Tiny Upward Shove*, is forthcoming.

CAConrad is the author of nine books of poetry and essays, the latest of which is *While Standing in Line for Death*.

Steve Erickson's tenth novel, *Shadowbahn*, is now in paperback. Erickson is a Distinguished Professor at the University of California, Riverside.

Karen Joy Fowler is the author of six novels and three short story collections. Her 2013 novel *We Are All Completely Beside Ourselves* won a PEN/Faulkner award and was shortlisted for the Man Booker prize.

Lev Grossman is the author of the *Magicians* trilogy and the former book critic and lead technology writer for *Time*. He is currently writing a King Arthur novel called *The Bright Sword*.

Terrance Hayes is a poet, educator, and 2014 MacArthur Fellow. His seventh book of poetry, *American Sonnets for My Past and Future Assassin*, will come out this summer.

Harmony Holiday is a writer, dancer, and archivist/myth scientist, as well as the author of *Go Find Your Father/A Famous Blues*, *Negro League Baseball*, and *Hollywood Forever*. She lives in New York and Los Angeles.

Mitra Jouhari is a comedy writer and performer based in Brooklyn. Her TV writing credits include *Three Busy Debras*, *High Maintenance*, *The President Show*, and *Miracle Workers*.

Owen King is the author of the novel *Double Feature* and co-author of the novel *Sleeping Beauties*. He lives with his wife, the novelist Kelly Braffet, in New York's Hudson Valley.

Yahia Lababidi is an Egyptian-American thinker, poet, and author of seven books, the latest of which, *Where Epics Fail: Aphorisms on Art, Morality, and Spirit*, will be published in fall 2018.

Sally Wen Mao is a poet and recipient of a 2017 Pushcart Prize. Her second book of poetry, *Oculus*, will be published in 2019.

Bill McKibben is a journalist, environmentalist and author. He is a founder of 350.org, an international climate coalition.

Rick Moody is a novelist, short story writer, and artist in residence at New York University. His most recent novel, *Gardens of North America*, was published in 2015.

Tracy O'Neill is the author of *The Hopeful*, a columnist at Catapult, and editor-in-chief of the literary journal *Epiphany*.

Raquel Salas Rivera is the 2018-2019 poet laureate of Philadelphia. Their most recent book, *lo terceraio/the tertiary*, was published in April 2018.

Martin Seay is the author of the novel *The Mirror Thief*. Originally from Texas, he lives in Chicago with his spouse, the author Kathleen Rooney.

Jim Shepard is the author of seven novels, the most recent of which is *The Book of Aron*, and five collections of stories, including *Like You'd Understand, Anyway*. He teaches at Williams College.

Kao Kalia Yang is a Hmong-American author, activist, teacher, and public speaker. Her third book, *A Map into the World*, will be published in 2019.

Matthew Zapruder is a poet, professor, translator, and editor. His most recent book, the essay collection *Why Poetry*, was published in 2017.

Please vote.

These organizations also deserve your support:

ADAPT
www.adapt.org

AFL-CIO
www.aflcio.org

AmeriCorps
www.americorps.gov

Everytown for Gun Safety
www.everytownresearch.org

Fair Immigration Reform Movement
www.fairimmigration.org

Fossil Free USA
www.gofossilfree.org/usa

League of Women Voters
www.lwv.org

National Resources Defense Council
www.nrdc.org

Need to Impeach
www.needtoimpeach.com

Peace Corps
www.peacecorps.gov

Report for America
www.reportforamerica.org

SAFE Cities Network
www.vera.org/projects/safe-cities-network

Taller Salud
www.tallersalud.org

Women's March
www.womensmarch.com